HUMILITY: THE BEAUTY OF HOLINESS.

IN TODAY'S ENGLISH AND WITH STUDY GUIDE

ANDREW MURRAY
GODLIPRESS TEAM

© **Copyright 2021 by GodliPress. All rights reserved.**

All rights reserved. The content contained within this book may not be reproduced, duplicated, or transmitted without direct written permission from the author or the publisher, except in the case of brief quotations embodied in critical articles or reviews.

Scripture quotations are from The ESV® Bible (The Holy Bible, English Standard Version®), copyright © 2001 by Crossway, a publishing ministry of Good News Publishers. Used by permission. All rights reserved.

"Humility" by Andrew Murray was first published in 1895. While holding firmly to Andrew Murray's classic teaching and theology and retaining the elegance of his writing style, this edition is updated to make Murray's writing more accessible to modern readers.

It includes the following updates:

- Unabridged, complete, and carefully updated text in modern English.
- A Study guide to ensure a deeper study of his original message.
- Updated organization and headings.
- An active table of contents.

CONTENTS

Introduction	v
Preface	ix
1. HUMILITY: THE GLORY OF THE CREATURE	1
Study Questions	5
2. HUMILITY: THE SECRET OF REDEMPTION	6
Study Questions	10
3. HUMILITY IN THE LIFE OF JESUS	12
Study Questions	16
4. HUMILITY IN THE TEACHING OF JESUS	17
Study Questions	22
5. HUMILITY IN THE DISCIPLES OF JESUS	23
Study Questions	27
6. HUMILITY IN DAILY LIFE	29
Study Questions	35
7. HUMILITY AND HOLINESS	37
Study Questions	41
8. HUMILITY AND SIN	43
Study Questions	48
9. HUMILITY AND FAITH	50
Study Questions	53
10. HUMILITY AND DEATH TO SELF	55
Study Questions	59
11. HUMILITY AND HAPPINESS	61
Study Questions	65

12. HUMILITY AND EXALTATION   66
    Study Questions   70

13. A PRAYER FOR HUMILITY   72

    About ANDREW MURRAY   75
    Notes   77

INTRODUCTION

Humility is something we all know we should have, or often think we have, but we struggle to hold on to. Most times, we don't even come close! Finding the right book to help understand and guide us is not easy, considering how many there are all telling us different techniques, ways, and plans.

Andrew Murray's *Humility* has become a classic in Christian literature. Applied in lectures, referred to in preaching, as personal guides, used in devotionals—it is cherished, loved, and respected by so many.

You will find tattered and worn copies of this book, only because they have been read more than once. Inside, there are notes and scribbles in the margins from readers trying to remember the treasures crammed into this little publication. Others keep it in their treasured collection alongside the likes of Bunyan, Lewis, Spurgeon, and Tozer.

Ask any preacher or teacher for their all-time favorite Christian books and this is one that will feature in most of those lists.

Why this book? Countless others have all tried to grasp and unlock the mystery of humility—autobiographies, self-helps, sermons, do-it-yourselfs, ancient manuscripts, allegorical tales—yet few stand out as classics like this. Very few find their way onto bookshelves in homes, offices, and churches around the world, translated into many languages, and read by people of all walks of life.

Andrew Murray's book, written more than 100 years ago, has survived to stand out above every modern take on the subject. Why? He does not flower his words with unnecessary stories or anecdotes, but asks the same straight questions we want to ask. And he provides answers! Through Biblical treatment of humility, he provides practical guidance for us to become more humble.

Murray's honest approach is what we need in a world where there is so much information and disinformation that it is often hard to know where the truth lies. But this book cuts directly through all of that, revealing a heart that is desperately in need of Jesus—the answer to the problem of pride.

As Christians, we all face the struggle of pride in its blatant arrogance and its subtle condescension. Often, the more we try and be humble, the more we fail, ending in a spiral of defeat. In this book, the quest for humility is laid out in simple terms; revealing to us the root of the problem right through to the glorious possibility of living such a life in Jesus.

An updated version is not changing or taking anything away from this classic, but allows today's readers the chance to understand what Andrew Murray was saying to all of us over a century ago. The heart and the spirit of the book are the same, just in English that we can grasp. To help even more, study questions have been added for you to think and discern about what is being said in each chapter.

In *Humility*, you will find refreshment for your spiritual walk and learn that humble dependence on God is the basis of all true blessing. You will learn to model your life after Jesus' life, find joy in serving, and add power to your witnessing. Bring your focus back to God and walk in His will as never before!

> Lord Jesus! May our Holiness be perfect Humility!
> Let Thy perfect Humility be our Holiness!

PREFACE

There are three great motives that inspire us to be humble. It defines me as a created being, a sinner, and a saint.

The first motive we see in the angels, in mankind before the fall, and in Jesus as Son of Man.

The second motive appeals to us in our fallen state and points out the only way we can return to our rightful place as part of God's creation.

In the third motive, we have the mystery of grace that, as we lose ourselves in the overwhelming greatness of God's love, humility fills us with everlasting contentment and worship.

In our ordinary religious teaching, the second aspect has been emphasized too often. Some have even gone to the extreme to say we must keep sinning if we are to stay humble. Others have said that living in condemnation is the secret of humility.

As a result, life for many Christians has missed the mark. They have not been properly shown their relation as created beings—nothing is more natural and beautiful and blessed than to be nothing—that God may be all. It has not been made clear that sin does not humble us the most, but grace. The person that is led out of their sinfulness to fully realize God as Creator and Redeemer is the one that will take the lowest place before Him.

In these thoughts that follow, I have placed much attention on the humility that defines us as created beings. Not only because the connection between humility and sin is so highlighted in all our religious teaching, but I also believe that for Christians to live a fulfilled life, it is vital to understand our own need for humility.

If Jesus is to be our example of humility, we need to understand what motivated Him to live that way. We must stand on the same ground if we are to become more like Him. If we are to be humble, not only before God but towards others —if humility is to be our joy— we must see that it is not only as the mark of shame because of sin. It should also be seen apart from sin, as a covering with the very beauty and joy of heaven and Jesus.

We will see that just as Jesus found His glory in becoming a servant, so He also said to us, *"Whosoever would be first among you, shall be your servant."* He simply taught us the truth that there is nothing so divine as being the servant and helper of all. The faithful servant who recognizes his position finds real pleasure in serving the master or his guests.

When we see that humility is something infinitely deeper than repentance, and accept it as sharing in the life of Jesus, we shall begin to learn that it is our true honor. We will find that being servants of all is the highest fulfillment of our destiny—human beings created in the image of God.

When I look back on my own experience or on the church, I am amazed at how few Christians seek humility as the defining feature in their walk to become disciples of Jesus. In preaching and living, daily activities of the home and social life, fellowship with Christians, the direction and performance of work for Christ—it is evident that humility is not valued as a vitally important virtue. However, it is the only root from which good character can grow, the one essential of true fellowship with Jesus.

Those who are seeking deeper holiness have not always done so with increasing humility. This is a loud call to all serious Christians to prove that meekness and lowliness of heart are the sign by which those who follow the meek and humble Lamb of God are known.

1

HUMILITY: THE GLORY OF THE CREATURE

'They cast their crowns before the throne, saying, "Worthy are you, our Lord and God, to receive glory and honor and power, for you created all things, and by your will they existed and were created.'
–Revelation 4:10-11.

God designed the universe to show the glory of His love, wisdom, and power so that those He created would be a part of His perfection and joy. God wanted to reveal Himself in and through created beings by showing as much of His goodness and glory as they could receive. But this was not for humanity to take hold of or discard as it wanted. No!

God is ever-living, ever-present, ever-acting. He holds all things by the word of His power, and in Him, all things exist. The relation of those He created to Himself could only be one of continual and complete dependence. As God created by His power, so he must always maintain everything by that same power. We only have to look back to the origin of existence to acknowledge that we owe everything to God. Our main concern, our highest good, and only happiness—now and forever—is to present ourselves as empty vessels where God can live in us and show His power and goodness.

The life God gives is not a single act but is continuously granted moment by moment through His mighty power. Humility—the place of total dependence on God—is the most natural duty and the highest good of the created being. It is the root of every virtue.

So pride, or the loss of this humility, is the root of every sin and evil. It was when the devil and his angels began to focus on themselves that they were led to disobedience, and were cast down from heaven. When the serpent breathed the poison of pride into the hearts of Adam and Eve—the desire to be as God—they also fell from their high position to the miserable place mankind now finds itself. In all of heaven and earth, pride and exalting yourself is the gate, the birth, and the curse of hell. (See Note A.)

Nothing can redeem us but the restoration of our lost humility. This is the original and only true relation of the creature to its God. So Jesus came to bring humility back to earth for us to share in it and be saved by it. In heaven, He humbled Himself to become a man. The humility we see in Him, He possessed in heaven; it brought Him to earth, and He brought it from heaven.

Here, '*He humbled himself by becoming obedient to the point of death,*' (Phil 2:8). His humility gave His death its value, and so became our redemption. The salvation He gives is nothing less than His life and death, His character and spirit, His own humility, as the foundation of His relationship to God and His redeeming work. Jesus took the place and fulfilled the destiny of man by His life of perfect humility. His humility is our salvation. His salvation is our humility.

So those of us who are saved must be stamped with the mark of being delivered from sin and fully restored to our original state. Our whole relationship with God and others is marked by complete humility.

Without this, we cannot remain in God's presence or experience His favor and the power of His Spirit. We cannot experience faith, love, joy, or strength. Humility is the only soil where Christ's character takes root in our lives, and every fault and failure can be linked to a lack of it. Humility is not just another good character quality, it is the root of all of them because we then have the right attitude before God, which allows Him to do as He desires.

God created us to think logically so that when we see our absolute need of His command for us to be humble, we will be ready and willing to obey. The church, though, has not fully understood the true nature and importance of this call.

It is not something we bring to God or something He gives us. Humility is simply realizing that we are nothing when we see how God is everything, and we make room for Him to be all in our lives. When we grasp that this is true nobility, and choose to be the empty vessel with all our will, mind, and emotions so God can work His life and glory in us, we see that humility is simply acknowledging what we were created for, and yielding to God His rightful place.

For true Christians who pursue holiness, humility should be the evident sign of their righteousness. This is often not so. Could the reason be that the teaching and example of the Church have never emphasized the importance of humility enough? This is because this truth has been neglected: Even though sin is a strong motive for humility, there is a more powerful one. The motive that makes the angels, made Jesus, makes the holiest saints so humble—the basis of our relationship to God, the secret of our contentment—is the humility and nothingness which leaves God free to be all.

I am sure there are many Christians who have had similar experiences of knowing the Lord for a long time without realizing that meekness and lowliness of heart should be the recognizable feature of a disciple as much as they were of the Master. Humility is not something that just takes place, but it must be desired through prayer, faith, and practice.

As we study God's Word, we will see very clear, repeated instructions Jesus gave to His disciples on this point. We will also see how slow they were to understand.

Right at the start, let us admit that there is nothing so natural to humans, so crafty and stealthy, so difficult and dangerous, as pride. Let us see that only a very determined and persevering seeking of God will show us how much we lack the grace of humility, and how useless we are to obtain it.

Let us study the character of Jesus until we are filled with love and admiration for His humility. And let us believe that when we are broken down under a sense of our pride, and our weakness to throw it off, Jesus Christ Himself will give us this grace as a part of His wondrous life within us.

STUDY QUESTIONS

After reading this first chapter, work through these study questions.

Take time to think about each one, search through the passage, then answer. If you are in a group, feel free to discuss and listen to other points of view. Don't rush onto the next question if you need more time to reflect and consider. These are merely to guide you to a deeper understanding of the text.

1. Why do you think God created humans?
2. How can we as created beings best demonstrate God's goodness and power?
3. Do you think it is possible for us to be truly obedient without humility?
4. Can a person have true humility without salvation?
5. According to this chapter, what is the root of all evil?
6. Murray says that humility is the root of all godly attributes and there is no faith, love, joy, or strength without it. Give three examples of why that is?

2

HUMILITY: THE SECRET OF REDEMPTION

'Have this mind among yourselves, which is yours in Christ Jesus, who, though he was in the form of God, did not count equality with God a thing to be grasped, but emptied himself, by taking the form of a servant, being born in the likeness of men.'
– Phillipians 2:5-7.

No tree can grow from another root. It can only live with the life that was in the seed it came from. The truth of this will help us understand the fall of Adam and the need to be redeemed through Jesus.

The Need. The devil was thrown down from heaven for his pride. His whole nature is pride. When he spoke words of temptation into Eve's ear, they were filled with the poison of hell. When she listened, and gave her desire and will over to the idea of knowing good and evil like God, the poison entered into her soul, blood, and life, destroying the wonderful humility and dependence upon God that would have been ours forever.

Instead, all of humanity became corrupted to its very root with the poison of Satan's own pride. All the misery of this world; wars and bloodshed among nations, selfishness and suffering, ambitions and jealousies, broken hearts and embittered lives, daily unhappiness, came from this curse. Either our own pride or that of others has brought us to this place.

It is because of pride that we need redemption. The only way to clearly see our need to be redeemed depends on us realizing the terrible nature of pride that has entered our being.

No tree can grow from another root.

The power that Satan brought into humans works daily and hourly, with mighty force throughout the world. We suffer because of it. They fear and fight and flee it, yet they do not know where it comes from, why it is so powerful. No wonder they do not know how to overcome it.

Pride's root and strength are spiritual, both outside as well as inside us. We need to confess it and hate it in our lives, and to see that it comes from the devil. If this causes us to feel like giving up ever getting rid of it, it will also drive us to the only supernatural power that can deliver us—the redemption of the Lamb of God. The desperate struggle against self and pride in us may seem hopeless when we think of the power of darkness behind it. But this will push us closer to realizing and accepting the power and life offered to us—the humility of heaven brought to us by the Lamb of God to cast out Satan and his pride.

No tree can grow from another root.

As we look at Adam and his fall to know the power of the sin within us, we need to know that Jesus, the Second Adam, has the power to give us a life of humility more real, lasting, and stronger than our pride. Our life is from Christ and in Christ. We are to walk *'rooted and built up in Him,' 'holding fast to the Head, from whom the whole body, nourished and knit together through its joints and ligaments, grows with a growth that is from God,'* (Col 2:7,19).

The life of God through Jesus when He came to earth is the root in which we are to stand and grow. The same power that worked when he was born and raised from the dead, works in us every day. Our only need is to study, and know, and trust the life that has been revealed in Christ is now ours. It waits for us to receive it, to let it take over our whole being.

It is important that we know who Christ is and what He represents. We especially need to understand the root of His character as our Redeemer: His humility. What was the act of Jesus emptying Himself to become a man? Humility. What is His life on earth in the form of a servant? Humility. And what is His death on a cross? Humility. *'He humbled himself by becoming obedient to the point of death, even death on a cross.'* What is His ascension to glory? Humility exalted to the throne and crowned with glory. *'He humbled Himself...therefore God highly exalted him,'* (Phil 2:8-9).

In heaven, where He was with the Father, in His birth, His life, His death, His sitting on the throne, it is nothing but humility. Christ is the humility of God in human form. It is eternal love humbling itself, putting on meekness and gentleness, to win, and serve, and save us. As love makes God the servant of all, so Jesus became humility in the flesh. Even on the throne, He remains the meek and lowly Lamb of God.

If this is the root of the tree, its nature must be seen in every branch, leaf, and fruit. If humility is the life of Jesus and the secret of His death, then the strength of our spiritual life depends on making humility the one thing we admire, ask for, and sacrifice all else for. (See Note B.)

Is it surprising that most Christian lives are often so feeble and fruitless when the root of the life of Christ is neglected and unknown? Is it strange that the joy of salvation is hardly felt, when the humility with which Jesus brought it, is not searched for? Only when we seek humility in Christ, that is the death of self; that gives up finding praise from others for the honor that comes from God, which counts itself nothing. That God may be all, that the Lord alone may be exalted—until this becomes our only joy, at any price, there is very little hope of a faith that will overcome the world.

If you have never thought of humility inside of you or around you, stop and ask yourself if you see much of the meek and lowly Lamb of God in those who follow Him. Think of the shortage of love, the disregard for the needs, feelings, and weaknesses of others. Think of all the sharp, hasty judgments and harsh words that are excuses for being honest. What about the tempers and irritations, bitterness, and estrangement that have their root in pride that looks after itself?

You will see how a dark pride creeps in almost everywhere, even amongst Christians. Ask yourself what the effect would be if everything towards others was guided by the humility of Jesus. Would you not cry for the humility of Jesus in you and all around you? Fix your heart on this lack of humility that has been revealed in looking at Jesus' life, character, and redemption, and you will begin to feel what Christ's salvation truly is.

Believers, study the humility of Jesus. This is the secret, the hidden root of your redemption. Sink into it deeper every day. Believe with your whole heart that Christ, God's gift, will enter in to live and work inside you too, and make you what the Father wants you to be.

STUDY QUESTIONS

Redemption is a key part of Jesus' plan for our lives.

Having read this chapter, follow these questions to help you think more on this subject. Make notes or discuss these points with others. If you can, find extra verses from the Bible to back up your views. This will really help you to grasp more about humility and its link to salvation as Murray has outlined.

1. Why do we need redemption?
2. Do you think that Adam's fault was simply disobeying God or wanting to be equal with Him and not submitting?
3. Is it possible for humility to come naturally to a Christian as pride does to a sinner?

4. According to Murray, the center and foundation of Christ's life on Earth was His humility. Do you agree?
5. If the result of pride is bitterness, judgment, bad temper, and lack of love, what are the fruits of humility?
6. What do you think of the sentence, "hasty judgments and harsh words that are excuses for being honest?" Has this ever happened to you? Are you guilty of this type of honesty?

3

HUMILITY IN THE LIFE OF JESUS

'I am among you as the one who serves.'
– Luke 22:27.

In the Gospel of John, we see the inner life of Jesus. Here, Jesus speaks often of His relation to the Father, what His motives are, and the power and spirit in which He acts. Though the word 'humble' does not appear, Jesus' humility is most evident in this book than anywhere else in the Bible.

We have already said that this grace is nothing but that simple acceptance of the created being to let God be all—surrendering to His working. As the Son of God in heaven, and as man upon earth, Jesus submitted completely, giving God all the honor and the glory. What He taught, He lived: 'He who humbles himself will be exalted,' (Luke 14:11). This is evident as the Bible says, *'He humbled Himself...therefore God highly exalted him,'* (Phil 2:8-9).

Listen to His words about His relationship with the Father. See how often Jesus uses the words 'not' and 'nothing' when talking about Himself. Paul says "not I" to show the same relationship he shared with Christ as Jesus did with His Father.

- *'The Son can do nothing of his own accord'* (John 5:19).
- *'I can do nothing on my own. As I hear, I judge, and my judgment is just, because I seek not my own will but the will of him who sent me'* (John 5:30).
- *'I do not receive glory from people'* (John 5:41).
- *'For I have come down from heaven, not to do my own will but the will of him who sent me'* (John 6:38).
- *'My teaching is not mine, but his who sent me'* (John 7:16).
- *'But I have not come of my own accord'* (John 7:28).
- *'I came not of my own accord, but he sent me'* (John 8:42).
- *'I do not seek my own glory'* (John 8:50).
- *'The words that I say to you I do not speak on my own authority'* (John 14:10).
- *'The word that you hear is not mine but the Father's who sent me'* (John 14:24).

These words show us the deep roots of Christ's life and work. They reveal how God was able to work His mighty redeeming work through Him. They show Jesus' state of heart as the Son of the Father. They teach us about the nature and life of salvation that Christ brought and now offers us. He was nothing, that God might be all. Jesus gave up His will and powers entirely for the Father to work in Him. What He said about His own power, His will, glory, and mission with all His works and His teaching, was "not I; I am nothing. I have given Myself to the Father to work. I am nothing; the Father is all."

This life of surrender, absolute submission, and dependence upon the Father's will was perfect peace and joy for Christ. He lost nothing by giving everything to God. God honored His trust and did everything for Him, and then raised Him up to His own right hand in glory. And because Christ humbled Himself like that, with God always with Him, He could humble Himself before men too, and be the Servant of all. His humility was simply surrendering Himself to God so that the Father could do whatever He wanted to do in Him. It did not matter what others said or did to Him.

It is with this attitude and spirit that the redemption of Christ is effective. It is so we will have the same nature that we are enabled to share in Christ. This is denying ourselves as He asks of us. It is recognizing that self has nothing good in it, except as an empty vessel for God to fill, our self may not be allowed any claim to be or do anything. This is obeying Jesus: Being and doing nothing of ourselves, that God may be all.

Here we have the root and nature of true humility. When we do not understand or aspire to this, our humility is superficial and weak. We must learn how Jesus is meek and lowly of heart. He teaches us where true humility finds its strength—knowing that God works all in all, and we must yield to Him in perfect submission and dependence. We admit to be and to do nothing of ourselves. This is the life Jesus came to reveal and to give—a life to God that came through death to sin and self.

If we feel that this kind of life is beyond our reach, it should drive us to seek it in Him. It is only Christ living this life inside of us that will bring humility. If we long for this, let us search for the secret of this goldy nature that is open to every child of God—that we are only vessels and channels through which God reveals His wisdom, power, and goodness. The root of godly character, faith, and real worship, is knowing that everything comes from God, then bowing in deepest humility to wait on Him for it.

Jesus' humility toward God and mankind was the spirit of His whole life, not just a passing feeling when He thought of the Father. He regarded Himself the Servant of God for those God made and loved. It was natural to consider Himself a servant for God to do His work of love through. He never thought of seeking honor or using His power to assert Himself. His whole spirit was a life yielded to God to work in.

We must understand the humility of Jesus as the center of His work of salvation, the glorified life of the Son of God, the true relationship to the Father, and the gift He gives for us to be with Him. Only then will we feel the burden of not having true humility and will set aside just being ordinary Christians to take hold of it.

Are you clothed with humility? Take a look at your daily life. Ask Jesus. Ask your friends. Ask the world. Begin to praise God that Jesus has begun to show you a heavenly humility that you hardly knew, and a blessing you have never tasted before.

STUDY QUESTIONS

This chapter really gives us a clear picture of humility—in the form of Jesus.

By working through these questions, refer back to what Murray says to help you in answering. It is very helpful and enlightening to read the verses from your own Bible and not just as they are listed in this book. This will help you to see them in context and even lead you to other connecting verses that give you a greater understanding of what is being said.

1. Are modesty and humility the same thing?
2. What is the difference between humbling yourself before others and humbling yourself before God?
3. Christ found perfect peace in submitting to His Father's will. Why do we as humans always find it easier to pursue our own will?
4. Can you think of a few practical ways that Jesus showed the humility He was talking about?
5. Do you agree with Murray that our 'self' has nothing good in it?
6. What do you think your friends and family would answer when asked whether you are clothed in humility or not?

4

HUMILITY IN THE TEACHING OF JESUS

'Learn from me, for I am gentle and lowly in heart.'
– Matthew 11:29.

'Whoever would be first among you must be your slave, even as the Son of Man came not to be served but to serve.'
– Matthew 20:27-28.

We have seen Jesus' humility through His own heart. Now, let us listen to His teaching. What does He say about it, and how far does He expect His disciples to follow His example? We will study the Bible through quotes to see how He taught humility so that we understand what He asks of us.

1. Look at the start of Jesus' ministry. In the Sermon on the Mount, He says, *'Blessed are the poor in spirit, for theirs is the kingdom of heaven...Blessed are the meek, for they shall inherit the*

earth,' (Matt 5:3,5). His very first words about the kingdom of heaven show us the only open gate through which we can enter. The kingdom comes to the poor, those who have nothing in themselves. The earth will belong to the meek, those who seek nothing in themselves. The blessings of heaven and earth are for the lowly. For the heavenly and the earthly life, humility is the secret of blessing.

2. *'Learn from me, for I am gentle and lowly in heart, and you will find rest for your souls,'* (Matt 11:29). Jesus tells us of the spirit we will find, learn, and receive in Him as our Teacher. He offers us meekness and lowliness where we shall find perfect rest for the soul. Humility will deliver us.

3. The disciples were arguing about who would be the greatest in the kingdom and asked the Master. Pointing to a child, He said, *'Whoever humbles himself like this child is the greatest in the kingdom of heaven,'* (Matt 18:4). The question of who is the greatest in heaven is a radical one. What will be the most honored position in the heavenly kingdom? No one but Jesus knew the answer. The highest glory of heaven, the true godly characteristic, is humility. *'For he who is least among you all is the one who is great,'* (Luke 9:48).

4. The sons of Zebedee had asked if they could sit on the right and left of Jesus, the most important places in the kingdom. Jesus said that only the Father could give those places to those for whom they were prepared. They must not look or ask for them. They should rather focus on the cup and the baptism of humiliation. And then He added, *'Whoever would be first among you must be your slave, even as the Son of Man came not to be served but to serve.'* (Matt 20:27-28) Humility is

the mark of Christ, and will also be the standard of glory in heaven. The place nearest to God is the lowliest. The prime position in the Church is promised to the humblest.

5. Speaking of the Pharisees and their love of the positions of honor, Christ said again to the crowds and the disciples (Matt. 23:11), *'The greatest among you shall be your servant.'* Humiliation is the only ladder to honor in God's kingdom.

6. At the house of a Pharisee, He told the parable of the guest who was invited to a better position (Luke 14:1-11) and added, *'For everyone who exalts himself will be humbled, and he who humbles himself will be exalted.'* The demand cannot be changed; there is no other way. Only the humble will be exalted.

7. After the parable of the Pharisee and the tax collector, Jesus spoke again (Luke 18:14), *'For everyone who exalts himself will be humbled, but the one who humbles himself will be exalted.'* In the temple and worship of God, everything that is not full of humility towards God and men is worthless.

8. After washing the disciples' feet, Jesus said (John 13:14), *'If I then, your Lord and Teacher, have washed your feet, you also ought to wash one another's feet.'* The authority of command and example make humility the first and most important feature of being a disciple.

9. At the Last Supper, the disciples still argued about who was the greatest (Luke 22:26-27). Jesus said, *'Rather, let the greatest among you become as the youngest, and the leader as one who serves. But I am among you as the one who serves.'* The path Jesus walked and opened up for us, the power and spirit in

which He worked salvation and saves us, is the humility that makes me the servant of all.

How little this is taught. How little it is practiced. How little the lack of it is felt or confessed. I am not saying that hardly anyone grows to become more like Jesus in His humility. But I say that only a few ever think of making something they desire or pray for. How little the world has seen it. How little has it been seen in the church.

'Whoever would be first among you must be your slave.' God wants us to believe that Jesus means this! We all know that a faithful servant or slave is devoted to the master's interests, taking care to please him, delighting in his prosperity, honor, and happiness. Some people have had these characteristics and to be called a servant was something to glory in.

Has it not been a new joy as Christians for many of us to know that we may surrender ourselves as servants and slaves to God? We have found that serving Him is true freedom—freedom from sin and self.

The next lesson to learn then is that Jesus calls us to be servants of one another. If we eagerly accept this, we will be blessed with even more freedom from sin and self. At first, it may be hard because of our pride, which still counts itself to be something. But when we learn that being nothing before God is the glory we were created for, the spirit of Jesus, the joy of heaven, we joyfully serve even those who are hard to love.

When our heart is set on this, we will find every word of Jesus on humility brings new excitement. No place will be too low, no stooping too deep, and no service too hard or too drawn-out if we have fellowship with the One who said, *'I am among you as the one who serves.'*

Brothers and sisters, the path to the higher life leads down, lower down! This was what Jesus said to the disciples who were thinking of being great in the kingdom, and of sitting on His right hand and His left. Do not look or ask to be lifted up, that is God's work. Humble yourselves, and take no place before God or man except as a servant—that is your work. Let that be your one purpose and prayer.

God is faithful. Just as water flows down to the lowest place, so the moment God finds someone humbled and empty, His glory and power flow in to lift up and bless. Humble yourself—that is our concern. Lifting people up and honoring them—that is God's concern. By His mighty power and in His great love, He will do it.

Sometimes, people talk as if humility and meekness will rob us of everything that is great and courageous. If only we would believe that by humbling ourselves and becoming a servant, we find the honor of the kingdom of heaven, the royal spirit of the King, a God-like character! This is the path to the joy and glory of Jesus living in us, His power in our lives.

Jesus, the meek and lowly One, calls us to learn about the path to God from Him. Let us study the words we have been reading until our hearts are filled with the need for humility. And let us believe that what He shows, He gives. What He is, He imparts. As the meek and lowly One, He will come in and live in the longing heart.

STUDY QUESTIONS

Jesus' own words to his disciples and us are very important in understanding humility.

These questions will help you to think, discuss, and understand more of what He was saying and calling us to. If you are able, find the same situations or words in the other gospels (Matthew, Mark, Luke, and John) to highlight these teachings even more.

1. What is your idea of a servant?
2. Christ calls us to be servants. What does he call us to be after that?
3. Is humility thinking less of yourself or thinking of yourself less?
4. Have you ever felt that being meek and humble might make you less bold and courageous?
5. To humble ourselves is our responsibility. What is God's responsibility?
6. Do you ever feel joy while serving others? Why?

5

HUMILITY IN THE DISCIPLES OF JESUS

'Let the greatest among you become as the youngest, and the leader as one who serves.'
– Luke 22:26.

We have looked at humility in Jesus and His teaching. Let us see it in His chosen followers—the twelve apostles. If we see any of them without humility, it will show us the contrast between Christ and the disciples more clearly. It will also highlight the change that Pentecost brought in them, and prove how real it is for us to be a part of the perfect triumph of Christ's humility over the pride Satan in each of us.

In the teaching of Jesus, we have seen the disciples and their lack of humility. Once, they had been arguing which of them should be the greatest. Another time, the sons of Zebedee asked for the places of honor—to the right and left of Jesus.

Again at the Last Supper, they squabble over who was the greatest again.

There were moments when they were humble before the Lord. Peter cried out, *'Depart from me, for I am a sinful man, O Lord,'* (Luke 5:8). The disciples all fell down and worshipped Jesus when He calmed the storm. But these few acts of humility are very obvious against the natural instinct of pride that they so often showed. When we analyze this, we learn important lessons.

First, we can see that even in a committed and active Christian, humility is still lacking. It's clear to see in the disciples. They were sincere and devoted to following Jesus and gave up everything to do so. The Father revealed to them that Jesus was the Christ of God. They believed in Him, loved Him, and obeyed His commandments. They left everything and stuck with Him even when others turned away. They were ready to die with Him.

But deeper than all this, there was a dark power. They were hardly aware of it or how disgusting it was. It had to be put to death and thrown out before they could observe Jesus' power to save. It is the same for us today.

We find professors and ministers, evangelists and workers, missionaries and teachers, who are blessing millions and are filled with the gifts of the Spirit. But when hard times of testing come or their lives are exposed, it is painfully clear that there is no humility to be seen. It confirms the fact that humility is one of the highest characteristics. It is also one of the most difficult to gain. We should focus all our efforts on achieving it. It is a grace that only comes in power through the Spirit when Christ lives within us.

Second, we see how weak teaching and personal effort are in conquering pride or acquiring a meek and lowly heart. For three years, the disciples had been learning from Jesus. He had taught them the main lesson: *'Learn from me, for I am gentle and lowly in heart,'* (Matt 11:29).

Time after time, He had spoken to them, to the Pharisees, to the crowds, of humility as the only path to the glory of God. Jesus had not only lived before them as the Lamb of God in divine humility, He had also revealed the inmost secret of His life to them: *'For even the Son of Man came not to be served but to serve,'* (Mark 10:45). *'I am among you as the one who serves,'* (Luke 22:27).

He had washed their feet and told them to follow His example. And yet, it had little effect. At the Last Supper, there was still the argument as to who should be greatest. No doubt they tried to learn His lessons, and not to disappoint Him again. But it was no use.

It is a lesson for them and us that no teaching, not even from Jesus can get rid of pride. No convincing argument, no wonderful ideas of humility, and no personal effort can do this. When Satan casts out Satan, he only enters again in a mightier, more hidden power. Nothing works, except a new heart in humility, completely takes the place of the old and becomes our very identity.

Third, we can only become truly humbled by Jesus in His divine humility living in us. Our pride came from someone else: Adam. Our humility must also come from someone else. Pride is ours and rules in us with such terrible power because it is our nature. Humility must be ours in the same way; it must be our very nature.

The promise is, *'where sin increased, grace abounded all the more,'* (Rom 5:20). All Jesus' teaching and the disciples' useless efforts were necessary for Him to enter into them with power and give them the humility they desired.

In His death, He destroyed the power of the devil and put away sin to bring salvation. In His resurrection, the Father gave Him a totally new life. The life of a man in the power of God so we could hear and understand Him and be filled and renewed by His power. In Jesus' ascension, He received the Spirit of the Father, to do everything He could not do while on earth.

He could make Himself one with those He loved, and live their lives for them. Then they could live in humility like His because Jesus lived and breathed in them. On Pentecost, He came and took possession of them. All the preparation and conviction, awakening desire and hope through His teaching, was completed by the mighty change the Holy Spirit brought. The lives and the letters of James, Peter, and John are evidence that it had all changed. The spirit of the meek and suffering Jesus had taken control of their lives.

I am sure all of us are in different stages in our understanding. Some have never thought much about this or realized how important it is in the life of a Christian. Others feel condemned because they have tried and failed. There are people who can share about the spiritual blessing and power they have received, but have not seen the need for humility like those around them. Still, others can say how the Lord has delivered and given them victory, as they have learned how much they still and can expect out of the fullness of Jesus.

Whichever stage you belong to, I urge you to seek a deeper conviction of the unique place that humility has in our life with Jesus. We must see that it is impossible for the Church or the believer to become like Him if humility is not seen as His greatest glory, His command to us, and our highest joy.

Let us see how far the disciples had come even though they lacked humility. Let us pray that other gifts will not satisfy us so much, that we forget that the absence of humility is the secret reason that the power of God cannot work in our lives. Like Jesus, when we know and show that we can do nothing of ourselves, then God will do all.

When Jesus living in us becomes a real experience, then the Church will put on her beautiful garments and humility be seen as the beauty of holiness.

STUDY QUESTIONS

This is a great chapter for us to see that the disciples struggled with similar issues to us, even though they were with Jesus.

When you work through these questions, take your time to assess where you are in relation to these followers of Christ. Can you see yourself in any of them or the situations they find themselves in? By doing this, you will not just be studying what Murray says, but allowing it to challenge your own life.

1. Do you think it is possible to love Jesus but still lack humility?
2. Why were the disciples unable to follow Christ's example of humility?
3. If pride is our sinful nature from Adam, how do we put off the old man and put on the new?
4. Personal effort is useless in acquiring humility—what can we do then?
5. What is the secret reason why the power of God cannot do its work in us?
6. Murray talks about different stages of understanding in the last part of this chapter. At which stage do you see yourself?

6

HUMILITY IN DAILY LIFE

'He who does not love his brother whom he has seen cannot love God whom he has not seen.'
– 1 John 4:20.

What revelation, that the way we love God is measured by our fellowship and love of others. If it does not stand this test, then our love for God is false.

It's the same with our humility. It is easy to think we humble ourselves before God. But humility towards others is the only proof that before God it is real. This is the test of whether humility is in our hearts if it has become our nature, and if we have laid down our reputation like Jesus or not. When humility has become more than the way we pray to God in His presence, but the very spirit of our life, it will manifest itself in how we behave to our brothers and sisters.

This is a vital lesson to learn. The only humility that counts is not the one we try to show before God in prayer, but the one we carry with us in our ordinary lives. The most insignificant parts of daily life are the tests of eternity because they prove what kind of spirit is really inside of us. In our most unguarded moments, we show and see what we are. To know the humble person, and how they behave, you must follow and watch their daily life.

Isn't this what Jesus taught? When the disciples argue who the greatest should be, the Pharisees longed for the best places at feasts and in the synagogues, or when He had given them the example of washing their feet; He taught His lessons of humility. Humility before God is nothing if it is not proved in humility before men.

It's the same in Paul's teaching.

- To the Romans, he writes:

'*Love one another with brotherly affection. Outdo one another in showing honor,*' (ROm 12:10). '*Live in harmony with one another. Do not be haughty, but associate with the lowly. Never be wise in your own sight,*' (Rom 12:16).

- To the Corinthians:

'*Love is patient and kind; love does not envy or boast; it is not arrogant or rude. It does not insist on its own way; it is not irritable or resentful,*' (1 Cor 13:4-5). There is no love without humility as its root.

- To the Galatians:

'*Through love serve one another,*' (Gal 5:13). '*Let us not become conceited, provoking one another, envying one another,*' (Gal 5:26).

- To the Ephesians, immediately after the three wonderful chapters on heavenly life:

'*With all humility and gentleness, with patience, bearing with one another in love,*' (Eph 4:2). '*Giving thanks always and for everything to God the Father in the name of our Lord Jesus Christ, submitting to one another out of reverence for Christ,*' (Eph 5:20-21).

- To the Philippians:

'*Do nothing from selfish ambition or conceit, but in humility count others more significant than yourselves. Let each of you look not only to his own interests, but also to the interests of others. Have this mind among yourselves, which is yours in Christ Jesus,*' (Phil 2:3-5).

- And to the Colossians:

'*Put on then, as God's chosen ones, holy and beloved, compassionate hearts, kindness, humility, meekness, and patience, bearing with one another and, if one has a complaint against another, forgiving each other; as the Lord has forgiven you, so you also must forgive,*' (Col 3:12-13).

It is in our relationships and treatment of one another that the true meekness of mind and the heart of humility are to be seen. Our humility before God has no value unless it prepares us to reveal the humility of Jesus to others. Let us see humility in daily life after hearing these words.

The humble man always tries to follow the rule, '*In humility count others more significant than yourselves. Let each of you look not only to his own interests, but also to the interests of others.*' If we ask, how can we count others better than ourselves when they are below us in wisdom, holiness, natural abilities, or grace? This kind of question proves how little we understand what humility of mind really is.

True humility comes when we see we are nothing and have decided to deny ourselves, to let God be all. If you have done this and can say, "I have lost myself to find God," then you no longer compare yourself to others. Then you have stopped thinking of yourself in God's presence. You will interact with other people knowing you are nothing, not looking for anything for yourself. You will be a servant of God and for His sake a servant of all.

A faithful servant might be wiser than the master, yet still has the true spirit and position of the servant. The humble person looks upon every child of God, even if they are weak and unworthy, and honors them as the son of a King. The spirit of Him who washed the disciples' feet makes it a joy to us to be the least, to be servants one of another.

The humble person feels no jealousy or envy. They can praise God when others are blessed instead of them. The humble person is happy when others are praised because in

God's presence they have learned, like Paul, to say, '*I am nothing,*' (2 Cor 12:11). They have received the spirit of Jesus, who did not look for honor or recognition.

We will often be faced with the temptation to become impatient, touchy, to think unkindly, or speak harshly. People fail, even Christians. But if we are humble, we will keep and live this in our hearts: '*Bearing with one another and...as the Lord has forgiven you, so you also must forgive,*' (Col 3:13). By putting on the Lord Jesus, we have put on '*compassionate hearts, kindness, humility, meekness, and patience,*' (Col 3:12).

Jesus has taken the place of self, and it will not be impossible to forgive as Jesus did. His humility is not just thinking or saying it. Paul says it's with '*a heart of humility,*' full of compassion, kindness, meekness, and long-suffering, that the sweet and gentle mark of the Lamb of God is seen.

As Christians, we sometimes focus on boldness, joy, contempt of the world, zeal, self-sacrifice. Pagans taught and practiced these things. The deeper, gentler, and holy characteristics that Jesus brought from heaven and taught are all linked to the cross and death of self—poor of spirit, meek, humble, and lowly. These are hardly thought of or valued.

We must put on a heart of compassion, kindness, humility, meekness, long-suffering, and show our Christ-likeness, not just to save the lost, but in every interaction with brothers and sisters—tolerating and forgiving just as He forgave us.

What does the Bible say about a humble person? Do others around us, people of the world, see those qualities in us?

Let's not settle for anything less than taking each of these verses as the promise of what God will work in our lives! These scriptures are what the Spirit of Jesus will birth inside of us.

Let's let each failure and mistake drive us humbly to the Lamb of God, knowing that on the throne of our hearts, His humility and gentleness will be streams of living water that flow from within us.

I say again, that we have no idea how the Church suffers because of a lack of true humility, not making room for God to prove His power. Christians find it hard to put up with and love others they don't get along with, they struggle to keep the unity of the Spirit in peace. Instead of working in joy together, they became a hindrance and a burden. All because they lack humility, which counts itself nothing and rejoices in being the least, only seeking, like Jesus, to be the servant and helper of others—even those who don't deserve it.

Why do people who joyfully give themselves up for Christ find it so hard to give themselves up for their brothers and sisters? Is it the Church's fault for not teaching enough that the humility of Christ is the most important characteristic of the Spirit? But let us not be discouraged. Seeing this lack of humility should stir us to expect more from God. Let us see every person who tests or annoys us, as God's grace and instrument to purify and exercise the humility of Jesus within us. And let us have faith that God is everything and we are nothing, that in God's power, we only seek to serve one another in love.

'I knew Jesus, and He was very precious to my soul: but I found something in me that would not keep sweet and patient and kind. I did what I could to keep it down, but it was there. I sought Jesus to do something for me, and when I gave Him my will, He came to my heart, and took out all that would not be sweet, all that would not be kind, all that would not be patient, and then He shut the door.' – George Foxe.

STUDY QUESTIONS

This chapter begins to outline practical and personal ways in which we can see and understand humility in our daily lives.

Before diving into the study questions, spend some time just looking over the verses that Murray has outlined from the letters of Paul to the churches in this passage. Each of them has significant meaning in the light of humility. Look them up in your Bible and read a few verses before and after to give you some context of what Paul was trying to say.

1. Can we be humble before God if we are not humble before man?
2. Do you think it is correct to say humility without work is dead?
3. If we are not naturally humble in our weakest moments, do we carry true humility?
4. Is there true love without humility?
5. What does our humility before God prepare us for?
6. To allow God to be all in our lives, what should we do?

7. What is a better virtue: contempt for the world or death of the flesh?

7

HUMILITY AND HOLINESS

'Who say, "Keep to yourself, do not come near me, for I am too holy for you.'
– Isaiah 65:5.

We hear a lot about Holiness: Those who seek after it, professors of holiness, teachings, and meetings. The truth of holiness in Christ and holiness by faith can be found in so many places. But the test of holiness that we seek and speak of will be seen in the humility it produces.

Humility is the one thing needed to allow God's holiness to live and shine through us. Jesus, the Holy One of God who makes us holy, showed us the secret of His life, death, and resurrection—divine humility. The test of our holiness will be our humility before God and men. Humility is the bloom and the beauty of holiness. False holiness is clearly seen in a lack of humility. Everyone who wants to be holy needs to be careful that what starts in the spirit does not end up in the flesh. Pride creeps in where we don't expect it.

A Pharisee and tax collector went to the temple to pray. The Pharisee will find a way to get into the most sacred place. Pride can lift its head in the very temple of God, and even worship can become all about self. The Pharisee can even disguise himself as a tax collector and confess sins as much as anyone who claims to be the holiest.

As we open our hearts to be the temple of God, these two men will come up to pray. The tax collector will find he is not in danger of the Pharisee next to him, who despises him, but the Pharisee inside him who compliments and praises him. In God's temple, when we think we are in the presence of His holiness, let us beware of pride. *'Now there was a day when the sons of God came to present themselves before the Lord, and Satan also came among them,'* (Job 1:6).

'God, I thank you that I am not like other men, extortioners, unjust, adulterers, or even like this tax collector,' (Luke 18:11). Even when we are thanking God for all He has done, self pats itself on the back. Even in the temple where we hear words of repentance and praise, the Pharisee will join in, and in thanking God be congratulating himself. Pride can dress up in the garments of praise or repentance.

Even though we don't agree with the words, *'I am not like other men'*, their spirit can be found in our feelings and language towards others. Just listen to the way in which Christians speak of one another. How little of the humility of Jesus is seen. Deep humility must be the keynote of everything the servants of Jesus say about themselves or each other.

How many churches, missions, or committees have had their peace broken and God's work set back because Christians have acted irritably, impatiently, in self-defense, with harsh judgments, said unkind words, did not put others first, and have shown hardly any humility in their holiness? There have been times of great humbling and brokenness, but it is not the same as being clothed with humility, having a humble spirit, having a mind that thinks as a servant of others as Jesus did.

"Stay clear, I am holier than you!" What a joke on holiness! Jesus, the Holy One, is the humble One—the holiest will be the humblest. There is no one holy but God—we have as much holiness as we have of Him. What's really of God will be our real humility, because humility is our self disappearing as we see that God is all. The holiest will be the humblest.

We don't often see the open boasting as in the Jews of Isaiah's day—our manners have taught us not to speak like those people. But the same spirit is still seen in the way other believers or the lost are treated. When opinions are given, work is done, and faults are exposed, even though they wear tax collector's clothes, the Pharisee's voice is still heard: '*God, I thank you that I am not like other men.*'

Can such humility be found where we count ourselves servants of all? Yes. '*Love is patient and kind; love does not envy or boast; it is not arrogant or rude. It does not insist on its own way,*' (1 Cor 13:4-5). Where the spirit of love is in our heart, where nature of Christ as the meek and lowly Lamb of God is formed in us, then the power of perfect love exists that forgets itself and finds joy in blessing others, bearing with them, and honoring them regardless of their weakness.

Where this love enters, God enters. And where God is present in His power and shows us who He really is, then we become nothing. When we become nothing before God, we cannot help being humble towards others. The presence of God is not here now and then gone the next, but it is a covering under which we constantly live. Its deep humility becomes the holy place that all our works and words come from.

May God teach us that our thoughts, words, and feelings about others are His test of our humility towards Him. May we learn that our humility before Him is the only power that enables us to always be humble before others. Our humility must be the life of Christ, the Lamb of God, inside us.

If you are teaching others about holiness or seeking it for your own life, be warned. Religious pride is the most subtle and dangerous pride. No one actually says, "Stay clear, I am holier than you!" But subconsciously, a secret habit of commending yourself as you compare how far you are to others can grow. You will not recognize it in obvious words and actions, but by the absence of one thing—a deep humility that marks the soul that has seen the glory of God (Job 42:5-6; Isa. 6:5).

This pride can be picked up by those with discernment in the tone of your voice and how you speak of others. Even the world notices and points to it as proof that Christians are no better than they are.

Let's hear this warning. Unless we increase in our desire for humility, we may find that we have been wasting our time on beautiful thoughts, feelings, and empty actions. The true mark of God's presence—the disappearance of self—was never there. Let us run to Jesus, and hide in Him until we are clothed with His humility. That is the only way to holiness.

'ME is a most demanding character, requiring the best seat and the highest place for itself, and feeling terribly wounded if its request is not recognized. Most of the quarrels among Christian workers arise from the demands of this gigantic ME. How few of us understand the true secret of taking our seats in the lowest rooms.'
– Hannah Whitehall Smith.

STUDY QUESTIONS

Holiness is something we often have an idea of but don't always fully understand. This chapter really opens our minds to see it in connection with humility.

As you work through each question, make notes, find extra verses from the Bible, and treat this time as a study and self-analysis in terms of what Murray has written. If you are unsure or don't agree with something—take your time and pray about it. Remember that it is one thing to study and understand, but it is another to allow God to work it into our hearts.

1. What do you think being holy means?
2. If you had to choose only one, which would you pick: holiness or humility? Why?
3. What is false holiness? Can you describe what it looks like in a person?
4. Murray talks about "wasting our time on beautiful thoughts, feelings, and empty actions." What does this mean? Have you been in this position before?
5. Murray says the "holiest will be the humblest." What do you think this means?
6. What is the warning for teachers? Why do you think this is the case?

8

HUMILITY AND SIN

'Sinners, of whom I am the foremost.'
– 1 Timothy 1:15

Humility is often identified with repentance and regret. As a result, the only way to increase in humility is by focusing on sin. By now, we should have learned that humility is something far more.

In Jesus' teachings and the disciples' letters, we see how often humility is introduced without mentioning sin. In the universe, how the created being exists before its Creator, and how Jesus lived and gave His life, humility is the core of holiness. It is denying self to allow God on the throne, where He is all and we are nothing.

Even though I want to make this point very clear, man's sin and God's grace give a new depth and intensity to the humility of Christians. Just look at Paul to see that even though he was living a holy and given life, he was completely aware of the sinner he had been.

He often refers to his time as a persecutor and blasphemer.

- 'For I am the least of the apostles, unworthy to be called an apostle, because I persecuted the church of God...On the contrary, I worked harder than any of them, though it was not I, but the grace of God that is with me,' (1 Cor. 15:9-10).
- 'To me, though I am the very least of all the saints, this grace was given, to preach to the Gentiles the unsearchable riches of Christ,' (Eph. 3:8).
- 'Though formerly I was a blasphemer, persecutor, and insolent opponent. But I received mercy because I had acted ignorantly in unbelief...Christ Jesus came into the world to save sinners, of whom I am the foremost,' (1 Tim. 1:13, 15).

God's grace had saved him. He remembered his sins no more. But Paul never forgot how terribly he had sinned. The more he rejoiced in God's salvation and how God's grace filled him with joy, the more aware he was of being a saved sinner. That salvation had no meaning or wonder unless the sense of his being a sinner made it precious and real to him. He could not forget that it was a sinner God had taken up in His arms and crowned with His love.

The verses we have just read are not Paul's daily confession of sin—that is clear if you study them carefully. They have a far deeper meaning. They refer to something that lasts forever, bringing deeper awe and worship to the humility in which those who are saved bow before the throne—washed from their sins in the blood of the Lamb. Even in glory, those who are saved will still be ransomed sinners. Christians cannot live in the full light of God's love without knowing that the sin they were saved from is their only claim to all that grace has promised to do in them.

As sinners, we came to God in humility. This humility develops a new meaning when we take it on as new creations. But its deepest, richest tones of adoration are always remembered in that moment of God's wondrous, redeeming love.

The full impact of Paul's verses is that through his whole Christian life, there is no confession of sin. There is no mention of shortcoming or defect, no suggestion that he has failed or sinned against the law of perfect love. Instead, he actually vindicates himself to the point of living a blameless life before God and men.

- *'You are witnesses, and God also, how holy and righteous and blameless was our conduct toward you believers,'* (1 Thess. 2:10).
- *'For our boast is this, the testimony of our conscience, that we behaved in the world with simplicity and godly sincerity, not by earthly wisdom but by the grace of God, and supremely so toward you,'* (2 Cor. 1:12).

This is not something he hopes for or wants to achieve someday, it is what his actual life had been. Whatever we may think about this, we have to admit, Paul lived a life in the power of the Spirit that is very hard to match.

My point is that Paul not focusing on confessing sins emphasizes that daily sinning will not bring us deeper humility. Instead, it was how he continually positioned himself in grace. Our place of blessing, our position before God, must be the same as those whose highest joy it is to confess that they are sinners saved by grace.

Paul remembered only too well his terrible past sins before he encountered God's grace and power that would keep him from sinning again. He also never forgot the dark hidden power of sin ready to come in, but held back by the presence and power of Jesus living in him.

'For I know that nothing good dwells in me, that is, in my flesh'—these words of Romans 7:18 describe our flesh to the end of our lives. The glorious deliverance of Romans 8:2—*'For the law of the Spirit of life has set you free in Christ Jesus from the law of sin and death'*—does not mean that the flesh is destroyed or made holy, but the Spirit continuously gives us victory as He puts to death the deeds of the body.

Health removes disease. Light swallows up darkness. Life conquers death. So, Jesus living in us through the Spirit is the health, light, and life of our souls. Our conviction of how helpless we are toughens our faith in the continual work of the Holy Spirit, giving us a humbled dependence on Him and bringing faith and joy as support to humility. This humility only lives by the grace of God.

The three verses above all show that it was the wonderful grace given to Paul, which he needed every moment, that humbled him so deeply. The grace of God helped him to work harder than the rest. The nature and glory of grace for sinners enabled him to preach to the lost about the riches of Christ. This grace was overflowing with faith and love in Jesus.

It was also this grace that kept Paul's consciousness of having sinned, and still capable of sin, so alive. *'Where sin increased, grace abounded all the more,'* (Rom 5:20). Grace deals with and takes away sin. The more we experience grace, the more conscious we are of being a sinner. It is not sin, but God's grace that will keep us humble. It is not sin, but grace that will make me see what sinners we are. Grace makes the place of deep humility the place I never leave.

I'm afraid there are many who have tried to humble themselves by condemning and criticizing themselves, but still sadly admit that they have come no closer to humility, along with kindness, compassion, meekness, and patience. Focusing on yourself, even with self-hatred, can never free us from self. It is the revelation of God, not only by the law-condemning sin, but by His grace delivering from it, that will make us humble. The law may break the heart with fear. It is only grace that works that sweet humility that becomes a joy.

It was the revelation of God in His holiness, drawing near to make Himself known in His grace, that made Abraham and Jacob, Job and Isaiah, bow so low. There will be no room for self in the soul that waits, trusts, and worships, and is filled with the presence of God the Creator as everything for the created being in its nothingness, and God the Redeemer in His grace, as everything for the sinner in his sinfulness. Only in this way can the promise be realized: *'And the haughtiness of man shall be humbled, and the lofty pride of men shall be brought low, and the Lord alone will be exalted in that day,'* (Isa 2:17).

It is the sinner living in the light of God's holy, redeeming love—experiencing the divine love dwelling inside through Jesus and the Holy Spirit—who cannot help but be humble. Not to focus on sin, but to focus on God, brings deliverance from self.

STUDY QUESTIONS

Dealing with sin in this chapter, Murray uses Paul as an example of what we might face in our own lives when trying to become humble.

Understanding Paul's struggle and acceptance of his situation will really help us to grasp this aspect of humility. These questions are simply a guide to help you to see this clearly for yourself. As you work through them, if you see something of your own struggles or weaknesses, write these down, spend time in prayer, and let God show you what He wants you to do.

1. Is sin doing wrong things or what is already in our hearts? (see Matt 5:27-28.)
2. What do you understand from the verse in Romans 5:20, *'Where sin increased, grace abounded all the more?'*
3. Why does Murray say that those who are *'condemning*

and criticizing' themselves are no closer to becoming humble?
4. Do you think there is a difference between repentance and regret?
5. Murray says that sin does not bring humility. Do you agree?
6. How can we be aware that we are sinners without becoming burdened by our sin?

9

HUMILITY AND FAITH

'How can you believe, when you receive glory from one another and do not seek the glory that comes from the only God?'
– John 5:44.

I heard someone say that the blessings of being a Christian were like objects in a shop window—you could clearly see them but not reach them. If you were told to reach out and take them, you would say that you can't because of the thick glass between you and the objects. Christians might see the promise of peace, love, and joy, yet feel there was something stopping them from obtaining these. What could it be? Pride.

The promises are so certain and free; the invitation so strong; God's power so available—only something in our hearts stops our faith from taking hold of the blessing. Jesus tells us it is pride that makes faith impossible. *'How can you believe, when you receive glory from one another?'*

Pride and faith are enemies. We will see that faith and humility are rooted together, and we can not have more faith than humility. We will see that we can have a strong conviction and know the truth while pride is in our heart, which makes faith, filled with God's power, impossible.

Isn't faith confessing we are nothing and helpless, surrendering and waiting for God to work? Isn't it the most humbling thing—accepting we depend on Him, unable to get or do anything He graciously gives? Humility prepares our hearts to live on trust. And even the smallest breath of pride —selfishness, arrogance, confidence in our own ability— only makes your flesh stronger. And flesh cannot enter the kingdom, or take hold of its blessings, because it refuses to allow God to be everything.

Faith allows us to see the spiritual world and its blessings. It seeks God's glory where he is everything. When we try to find glory from each other, loving and guarding the glory of this world, the honor and reputation from people, we cannot receive the glory that comes from God. Pride makes faith impossible.

Salvation comes through a cross and a crucified Christ. Salvation is fellowship with the crucified Christ in the Spirit of His cross. Salvation is being one with and delighting in the humility of Jesus. No wonder our faith is so weak when pride still rules us. Are we longing and praying for humility as the most important and blessed part of salvation?

Humility and faith are more closely linked in the Bible than many realize. We see it on two occasions when Jesus spoke of great faith. The centurion who said, '*Lord, I am not worthy to have you come under my roof,*' amazed Jesus enough to say, '*I tell you, with no one in Israel have I found such faith!*' (Matt 8:8-10). And the mother who said, '*Yes, Lord, yet even the dogs eat the crumbs that fall from their masters' table*' caused Him to reply, '*O woman, great is your faith!*' (Matt 15:27-28). Humility brings a person to be nothing before God, removing every obstacle to faith, only fearing that it is not completely trusting Him.

Isn't this the reason we fail in our pursuit of holiness? Isn't pride what made our dedication and faith so shallow and brief? We had no idea how much pride and self were still secretly working within us, and how only God by His power could cast them out. We didn't understand how a new heart needs to take the place of our old self to really make us humble. We didn't know that complete humility must be the root of every prayer, every approach to God, and all our dealings with people. We might as well try seeing without eyes, or living without air, if we think we can believe, draw close to God, or live in His love, without humility.

We have all made the mistake of striving to believe when our old self in its pride always stopped us from reaching God's blessings. No wonder we could not believe. We need to change direction. First, we need to humble ourselves under the mighty hand of God—He will exalt us. The cross, death, and the grave where Jesus humbled Himself, were His path to the glory of God. We have the same path. Let our desire and prayer be to humble ourselves as he did. Let us gladly accept whatever can humble us before God or others. This is the only path to the glory of God.

What about those who seem blessed or are a blessing to others, but have no humility? Is their faith strong, even though they clearly seek honor from those around them? With whatever special gifts they have been given, they will be a blessing only in proportion to the measure they believe. But even there, their faith is restricted, and the blessing they have is shallow and temporary because of their lack of humility.

A deeper humility would bring a deeper and fuller blessing. If they listened to the Holy Spirit, and not just performed works in His power, they would understand the fullness of grace and humility as the true life of power and holiness.

'How can you believe, when you receive glory from one another?' Nothing can cure you of wanting honor from others or feeling hurt when none is given, except seeking the glory from God. Let the glory of the all-glorious God be everything to you. You will be freed from the glory of men and of self, and be content and glad to be nothing. From this you will grow strong in faith, giving glory to God, and you will find that the deeper you sink in humility before Him, the nearer He is to fulfill every desire of your faith.

STUDY QUESTIONS

We often hear of faith, but very seldom in connection with humility. In this chapter, Murray really opens our eyes to see how deeply they are linked.

Using these questions to direct you, see what your view on faith is. What does the Bible say about it? Then bring these back to what Murray has written. By taking this approach of studying, you can gain a greater understanding of the relationship between faith and humility for your own life.

1. Murray talks about the promises of God. What are these promises?
2. What is your definition of faith? (see Heb 11:1.)
3. Why are pride and faith enemies?
4. What two occasions are quoted to show how closely faith and humility are linked?
5. "We have the same path." What does this phrase by Murray mean for us in this chapter?
6. What do you think about the passage about those who seem to be blessed or might be seen as a blessing to others but have no humility? Do you agree?

HUMILITY AND DEATH TO SELF

'He humbled himself by becoming obedient to the point of death.'
– Phillipians 2:8.

Humility is the path to death. In death, it becomes perfect. Humility is the blossom; death to self is the fruit. When Jesus humbled Himself to death, he opened a path for us to follow. There was no other way to totally prove His surrender to God or to rise above His human nature to the glory of the Father but through the cross. It is the same for us.

Humility must lead us to die to ourselves. That is how we prove we have completely given ourselves up to God. That is how we are freed from our sinful nature and find life in God. That is where we receive a new heart, where humility breathes life and joy.

We have talked about Jesus giving His disciples resurrection life. Through the Holy Spirit, the Lamb of God came to live in them. He won the power to do this by dying. The life He gave came from His death—Jesus' life surrendered and won through death. The One who lived in them was the One who was dead but now lives forever. His life, person, and presence bear the marks of a life born out of death. The same marks are in the life He gave His disciples. Only as the One who was crucified lives and works in the heart, can the power of His life be known.

Humility is the mark of death that shows a true follower of Jesus. Only humility leads to perfect death. Only death perfects humility. Humility and death are linked: humility is the bud; in death, the fruit is ripened to perfection.

Humility leads to perfect death—giving up self and becoming nothing before God. Jesus humbled Himself and became obedient to death as proof of having given up His will to the will of God. In dying, He gave up self, with its natural reluctance to drink the cup. He gave up the life He had taken as a human. He died to self and the sin that tempted Him. As man, He entered into the perfect life of God. If He had not been completely humble and counted Himself as nothing except as a servant to do the will of God, He never would have died.

So, how can I die to myself? Jesus gives us the answer. In Christ, you are dead to sin. The life in you has gone through death and resurrection. You are definitely dead to sin. But to have the full power of this death in your character depends on how much you allow the Holy Spirit to work Jesus' death in you. If you want this, humble yourself.

This is your one duty: Come before God helpless, admit you can't put your old life to death or bring life to yourself, sink into your own nothingness, surrender to God. Accept every humiliation, look at every irritation as a tool of grace to humble you. Use every opportunity of humbling yourself before others as a help to stay humble before God. God will accept this as proof that your whole heart desires it. He will use it to prepare you by the strengthening of the Holy Spirit to reveal Christ in you. Then, Jesus will be formed in you as a servant living in your heart. This is the path of humility leading to perfect death—the full and perfect experience that we are dead in Christ.

This death leads to perfect humility.

Many have made the mistake of wanting to be humble, but afraid to be too humble. They have many reasons, excuses, and questions about humility, and they never get around to completely surrendering themselves. Watch out that you don't do the same! Humble yourself to death. In dying to yourself, humility is perfected. Make sure that every experience of grace, each step toward holiness, becoming more like Jesus, that in your attitude and actions, death to self is evident to God and others.

Unfortunately, we can talk about a crucified life and a spiritual walk, while those closest to us still see much self in us. The sure sign that you have died to yourself is humility. It has no reputation, is empty of itself, and takes the form of a servant. Unfortunately, we can also speak about having a relationship with Jesus, who was despised and rejected, and of taking up His cross, while the gentle humility of the Lamb of God is not seen or even a priority. The Lamb of God is both humility and death—they are inseparable. We must receive Him in both forms so that they are in us too.

We would get nowhere if this was up to us to accomplish! Flesh can't overcome flesh, even with the help of grace. Self can't cast out self, even in a born-again believer. Praise God! The work has been done, finished, and perfected forever. The death of Jesus is our death to self. And when He ascended forever into the Holiest place, He opened the way for the Holy Spirit's power to work so the power of the death-life could be ours.

Following in the steps of Jesus in the pursuit of humility, we begin to hunger for something more. Our desire and hope are stirred, our faith becomes stronger, and we learn to look up and receive the fullness of the Spirit of Jesus. This fullness has the power to put our sin and selves to death every day. It also makes humility the all-pervading spirit of our life. (See Note C.)

> *'Do you not know that all of us who have been baptized into Christ Jesus were baptized into his death?... So you also must consider yourselves dead to sin and alive to God in Christ Jesus...present yourselves to God as those who have been brought from death to life,' (Rom 6:3,11,13).*

The thinking of a Christian should be filled by the same Spirit that brought Jesus to the cross. Before God, they must be as having died and raised to life again in Christ, carrying the mark of the crucified Lord. Death to self and sin, as well as the resurrection power of Jesus, should be evident in their lives.

Believer, claim the death and the life of Jesus as your own in faith. Through His death, find rest from self—the rest of God. Jesus committed His spirit into the Father's hands, so humble yourself each day into perfect dependence on God. He will raise you up and honor you.

Every morning, sink into the grave of Jesus. Every day the life of Jesus will be evident in you. Let a willing and happy humility be the mark that you have claimed your birthright of being baptized into the death of Christ. *'For by a single offering he has perfected for all time those who are being sanctified,'* (Heb 10:14). If we enter into His humiliation, we will find His power to die to ourselves, and to walk in humility, serving one another in love. Death to self is seen in humility like Jesus had.

STUDY QUESTIONS

Dying to yourself is not always properly understood, but in this chapter, Murray really makes it clear in terms of humility.

Instead of just working through these questions, spend time reflecting on your own life. How do you match up in terms of what is being said? If you are brave enough to discuss this with others, you can ask them to answer that question for you. This is not always easy to hear, but sometimes good for our own growth.

1. How can humility become perfect in death?
2. What do you think it means to die to yourself? Try and give some examples.
3. Why do you think some are "afraid to be too humble?"
4. Why does Murray mention those "closest to us" as seeing whether we have truly died to ourselves or not?
5. The chapter mentions that "flesh can't overcome flesh" and "self can't cast out self." Why do you think this is?
6. How often should we die to ourselves? (see Luke 9:23.)

11

HUMILITY AND HAPPINESS

'Therefore I will boast all the more gladly of my weaknesses, so that the power of Christ may rest upon me. For the sake of Christ, then, I am content with weaknesses, insults, hardships, persecutions, and calamities. For when I am weak, then I am strong.'
– 2 Corinthians 12:9-10.

To keep Paul from becoming proud because of the revelation he had been shown, he was also given a thorn in the flesh to keep him humble. He first wanted it removed, and he asked God three times. God's answer was that the trial was a blessing. In the weakness and humiliation, it brought, the grace and strength of the Lord would become real. Paul immediately changed his view, and instead of simply enduring or asking for the thorn to be taken away, he took pleasure in it. He had learned that humiliation is the place of blessing, power, and joy.

Every Christian that pursues humility goes through the same two stages: First, we fear, pull back, and ask for a way out. We have not yet learned to seek humility at any cost. We have accepted the command to be humble, and want to obey, but fail. We pray seriously for humility, but secretly wish to not go through anything that will make us humble. We are so in love with humility as the beauty of the Lamb of God, and the joy of heaven, that he would give up everything to have it.

In seeking and praying for it, there is still a burden and of bondage. To humble ourselves hasn't become the spontaneous expression of a life and character that is really humble. It hasn't become our joy and only pleasure. We can't say, "I am glad to boast in weakness, I am grateful for whatever humbles me."

Can we ever reach this place? Definitely! What can get us there? The same thing that brought Paul there—a new revelation of the Lord Jesus. Only He can show and remove self. Paul saw clearly that the presence of Jesus will banish every desire to seek anything of ourselves. Only Jesus can make us glad to accept every humiliation that will make us more like Him. These trials help us in the presence and power of Jesus, to choose humility as our highest blessing. Let us learn from Paul's example.

Many Christians, teachers, and leaders have learned the lesson of humility in weakness. We can see in Paul how he saw the danger of becoming proud. He needed to still learn what it was to be nothing; to die, that Christ might live in him; to take pleasure in his trials. He had to learn that to become more like Jesus, he had to empty himself and take joy in his weakness for God to be everything.

The greatest lesson a Christian must learn is humility. There may be dedication, passion, and spiritual experiences, but if the Lord does not work His way in you, you could still become proud. Holiness is humility. It only comes through Jesus' special dealings in our hearts.

If we look at our own lives in the light of Paul's experience, we will see if we glory in weakness, take pleasure in suffering. Have we learned to take criticism, injury, trouble, or difficulty as opportunities to show Jesus is everything to us? Is our own comfort and honor nothing, but humiliation the only thing we take pleasure in? It's a great blessing to be so free from self that whatever is said of us or done to us is lost and swallowed up in the thought that Jesus is everything.

Let's trust Jesus to deal with as He did with Paul. Paul needed discipline and instruction to learn what was more precious than the revelation he had been given—to glory in weakness and humility. We need the same lesson so much. Jesus will take care of us the same way to keep us from lifting ourselves up. If we do become proud, He will show us and deliver us from it.

Through trials, weakness, and suffering, He will bring us low, until we learn that His grace is enough for us to take pleasure in the things that keep us humble. His strength working in our weakness, and His presence filling our emptiness are the secret of humility that never fails. Then, just like Paul, we can say, *'For I was not at all inferior to these super-apostles, even though I am nothing,'* (2 Cor 12:11). His trials led him to true humility that boasts and takes pleasure in all that humbles.

'Therefore I will boast all the more gladly of my weaknesses, so that the power of Christ may rest upon me. For the sake of Christ, then, I am content with weaknesses.' The humble Christian has learned the secret of being content. The weaker you feel, the lower you sink, and the greater your trials, the more the power and the presence of Jesus are yours where you are nothing. The word of God brings a deep joy: *'My grace is sufficient for you,'* (2 Cor 12:9).

These two lessons show us that the danger of pride is greater and nearer than we realize—the grace for humility too.

It's in our richest, most blessed times, that the danger of pride is the greatest. The preacher whose congregation hangs on every word, the one teaching the secrets of heavenly life, the Christian sharing a testimony, the evangelist winning over the lost—they are all in danger. Paul was in danger without knowing it. What Jesus did for him is written so that we may recognize our own danger and see our only safety.

Rather than saying that someone who proclaims Jesus is full of himself or doesn't practice what he preaches, we can say that Jesus, in whom we trust, can make each of us humble. Grace for humility is also greater and nearer than we think. The humility of Jesus is our salvation: He is our humility. Our humility is His concern and His work. His grace is enough for us to meet the temptation of pride. His strength will be perfected in our weakness. Let us choose to be weak, to be low, to be nothing. Let humility be a joy and gladness to us. Let us take pleasure in the weakness that can humble us. The power of Christ will rest on us.

Jesus humbled Himself, so God honored Him. Jesus will humble us, and keep us humble. Let's agree and joyfully accept that. The power of Christ will rest on us. We will find that humility is the secret of true happiness and joy that nothing can destroy.

STUDY QUESTIONS

To be happy in Jesus is often something we take for granted without thinking about what it really means. This chapter opens our eyes to see it very differently through Paul's life.

Let these questions challenge you. Rather than answering them quickly and moving on, spend some time really looking at where you stand on each one. Is there room to understand more, to grow more, to allow the Lord to work more? Write your responses down—this is very helpful as we can often forget moments of clarity like this.

1. What did happiness mean to Paul?
2. What does boasting in your weakness mean to you?
3. The Bible does not really say what Paul's thorn was. What do you think it could have been after reading the verses? (2 Cor 12:7-9.)
4. Can you think of any 'thorns' in your own life?
5. Do you think going through hard trials and suffering has any part in God's plan for us?
6. Is it possible to find joy through pain and hardship?

12

HUMILITY AND EXALTATION

How am I to conquer this pride? Simple. Two things are needed: Do what God says you should—humble yourself. Trust that He will do what He should: honor you.

The command is to humble yourself. That doesn't mean you must conquer and get rid of your pride and form Jesus' humility in yourself. No, that is God's work. In honoring you, He lifts you up in the character of Jesus.

The command does mean you have to grab every opportunity of humbling yourself before God and man. With faith in the grace working in you, being sure of the victory you will have in grace, allowing Him to light up any pride of the heart, even though there will be failures, stand firm on this command: humble yourself.

Gratefully accept whatever God allows—inside or outside, friend or enemy, natural or spiritual—to remind and help you in being humbled. Think of humility as the most important godly character, your first duty to God, and protection of your heart. Set your heart on it, it's the source of blessing. God has promised that whoever themselves will be lifted up. Just do what God asks: humble yourself. He will do what He promised. He will give you grace and honor you.

God's dealings happen in two stages. The first is a time of preparation. His command and promise train and discipline us for something greater. Here, we experience effort and weakness, failure and partial success, and a hunger to become more like Jesus. Then comes the time of fulfillment. Faith takes hold of the promise and enjoys what it had so often struggled for in vain. This is true for every Christian as they seek Godly character.

God always acts first when it comes to our redemption. When that has been done, it's our turn. In the struggle to obey and fulfill our duty, we learn our weaknesses. In desperation we die to ourselves, to be equipped and ready to receive the promise of God. He began the work before we even knew Him or understood His purpose, but now we desire and welcome Him as the end, as everything.

It is the same when we pursue humility. God's command for every Christian: humble yourself. When we listen and obey, we are rewarded—yes, rewarded—with a painful discovery. Firstly, our deep pride we were unaware of—unwilling to consider ourselves or be considered as nothing, and reluctant to submit to God. Secondly, how weak our efforts and prayers are to destroy the hideous monster. If we learn to put our hope in God, and, despite the pride inside us, persevere in acts of humility before God and Men, we will be blessed.

Actions produce habits, habits breed attitude, attitude forms the will, and the rightly-formed will is character. It is the same with grace. Just as repeated actions become habits and attitudes, strengthening the will, He works with His mighty power and Spirit.

The humbling of a proud heart that is brought before God in repentance is filled with grace, has been conquered by Jesus, and brought a new character in it to maturity. The meek and lowly Jesus lives in this heart forever.

Humble yourselves in the sight of the Lord, and He will honor you. What is this honor? The highest privilege of the created being is to be a vessel to receive, enjoy, and show the glory of God. We can be this vessel if we are willing to be nothing so that God may be everything. Water always fills the lowest places first. The lower and emptier a man bows before God, the quicker and fuller God's glory will flow in.

The honor God promises is not an external thing. All He gives is more of Himself. It is not a trophy that has little to do with why it is being awarded. No, it is the effect and result of the humbling of ourselves. It is the gift of conforming to and taking hold of the humility of the Lamb of God. A proper reward for allowing God to completely come inside our hearts.

If we humble ourselves, we will be lifted up. Jesus is proof of this and a guarantee for it to happen to us. Let us take His yoke on us and learn from Him, for He is meek and lowly of heart. If we are willing to lower ourselves to Him, as He did for us, He will come down to our level again, and we will be equally yoked with Him.

As we enter deeper into the fellowship of His humiliation, and humble ourselves or are being humbled by others, we can be sure that the Spirit of God will rest on us. The presence and the power of Jesus will come to those that have humble spirits. When God takes His proper place in us, He will lift us up.

As you humble yourself, make His glory your priority. He will make your glory His priority as He perfects your humility. He will breathe into you the Spirit of His Son. As the life of God fills and takes control of you, there will be nothing so natural and sweet as to be nothing. There will be no more thought or wish for yourself because everything is occupied with Him who fills all. *'Therefore I will boast all the more gladly of my weaknesses, so that the power of Christ may rest upon me,'* (2 Cor 12:9).

Brothers and sisters, isn't this the reason that our dedication and faith have hardly helped in our pursuit of holiness? It was because self and its strength were working in the name of faith. God was only needed for self and its happiness. Self and its own holiness made us happy. We never knew that absolute, abiding, Christlike humility filling and marking our life with God and man, was the most essential element of a holy life that we were looking for.

It is only in finding God that I lose myself. Only in full sunshine can you see a small speck of dust. The same with humility as we come into God's presence to be nothing but a small speck in the sunlight of His love.

> 'How great is God! How small am I!
> Lost, swallowed up in Love's immensity!
> God only there, not I.'

May God teach us to believe that to be humble, to be nothing in His presence, is the highest achievement, and the greatest blessing of the Christian life. He says to us: '*I dwell in the high and holy place, and also with him who is of a contrite and lowly spirit,*' (Isa 57:15). May this be our destiny!

> 'Oh, to be emptier, lowlier,
> Mean, unnoticed, and unknown,
> And to God a vessel holier,
> Filled with Christ, and Christ alone!'

STUDY QUESTIONS

In this final chapter, Murray brings humility and honor to their proper places and allows us to see each one's place in relation to the other.

By now, if you have been using these study questions to guide you into more thought and discussion, you will know that using a book to make extra personal notes, reading the verses in their context in the Bible, and giving yourself time to see it all in relation to your own life, are good methods of gaining a better understanding of each topic.

1. What are the two ways needed for pride to be conquered?
2. Twice in this book, Murray uses the picture of a vessel and water flowing down to the lowest point. What do you make of this analogy?
3. Why is being honored so important to us as people?
4. What is meant by Jesus honoring/lifting you up?
5. It says, "make His glory your priority," can you think of examples and ways that this is possible?
6. After reading this book, what is your view on humility?
7. How attainable do you think it is for your life right now?

13

A PRAYER FOR HUMILITY

I will give you a perfect standard to measure what is true: Draw back from the world and all conversation for one month—don't write, read, or debate anything with yourself, stop the dealings of your heart and mind. With all the strength of your heart, lift up this prayer to God as often as you can for this month. Try on your knees, but even if you are sitting, walking, or standing, have a longing as you earnestly pray this one prayer to God:

'Heavenly Father, may Your great goodness be known to me. Take from my heart every kind and degree of pride, if it's from evil spirits or my own corrupt nature. Awaken in me the deepest depth and truth of humility that can make me worthy of being Your servant, a vessel through which You can display the riches of Your wisdom, power, and goodness.'

Reject every thought except to wait and pray from the bottom of your heart, with such truth and sincerity as those in torment wish to pray and be delivered from it. If you can and will give yourself up in truth and sincerity to this spirit of prayer, I will say that if you had twice as many evil spirits in you as Mary Magdalene had, they will all be cast out of you, and you will be forced to weep tears of love at the feet of Jesus as she did.

ABOUT ANDREW MURRAY

Andrew Murray always wanted to be a minister. But as a young man, it was not an act of faith that led him to theological college—simply a career choice. Only after completing his studies and graduating did he write these words in a letter to his parents: "Your son has been born again... I have cast myself on Christ."

Andrew Murray was born in South Africa on May 9, 1828. At the age of ten, he went to study under his uncle in Scotland. He completed his master's degree before continuing with theological studies in Holland, where he was ordained into the Dutch Reformed Church in 1848. Murray returned to South Africa as a minister to Dutch-speaking farmers. In this time, he married Emma Rutherford, and together they had eight children.

During his time in South Africa, he pastored churches in Worcester, Cape Town, and Wellington. He was pivotal in founding the Stellenbosch Theological Seminary, Grey's College, the Huguenot Seminary for young women, and Wellington Missionary Training Institute. Six times, he was nominated to the Dutch Reformed Synod. Murray traveled extensively as an evangelist and conference speaker, and was awarded honorary doctorates and other accolades for his work.

Andrew Murray is best known for his published works, which have become a staple diet of serious Christians throughout the world. Out of 240 works of his, classics like *Abide with Me, With Christ in the School of Prayer,* and *Absolute Surrender* stand out as favorites.

He died on January 18, 1917, leaving behind a rich legacy of solid biblical theology, an intimate relationship with God, and an inspiration to all believers that such a life in Christ is possible.

"May not a single moment of my life be spent outside the light, love, and joy of God's presence."

NOTES

NOTE A

"Pride can degrade the highest angels into devils, and humility can raise fallen flesh and blood to the thrones of angels. So, this is the great end of God raising a new creation out of a fallen kingdom of angels. For this reason, it stands in its state of war between the fire and pride of fallen angels, and the humility of the Lamb of God. It is here that the last trumpet may sound the great truth through the depths of eternity: that evil can only begin in pride and only end in humility.

The truth is that pride must die in you, otherwise, nothing of heaven can live in you. Under the banner of the truth, give yourself up to the meek and humble spirit of Jesus. Humility must sow the seed, or nothing will be reaped in Heaven. Do not look at pride only as a temper, nor at humility as a decent character. The one is death, and the other is life; the one is all hell, the other is all heaven.

As much as you have pride within you, you have the fallen angels alive in you. As much as you have true humility, so you have the Lamb of God within you.

If you could see what every stirring of pride does to your soul, you would beg anyone to tear it from you, even if it caused the loss of a hand or an eye. If you could see what a sweet, divine, transforming power there is in humility, how it expels the poison of your nature and makes room for the Spirit of God to live in you, you would rather wish to be the footstool of all the world than not have the smallest part of it." –Spirit of Prayer, Pt. II. p. 73, Edition of Moreton, Canterbury, 1893.

NOTE B

"We need to know two things:

1. That our salvation consists completely in being saved from ourselves, or what we are by nature.

2. That in the nature of things, nothing else could be our salvation or savior but the humility of God beyond all expression. So, the first unavoidable term of the Savior to fallen man: *Except a man denies himself, he cannot be My disciple,* (Matt 16:24). Self is the whole evil of fallen nature; self-denial is our capacity of being saved; humility is our savior. Self is the root, the branches, the tree, of all the evil of our fallen state.

All the evils of fallen angels and men have their birth in the pride of self. On the other hand, all the virtues of the heavenly life are the virtues of humility. It is humility alone that makes the unpassable gulf between heaven and hell. What is the great struggle for eternal life? It all lies in the strife between pride and humility: pride and humility are the two master powers, the two kingdoms in strife for the eternal possession of man. There never was, nor ever will be, but one humility, and that is the one humility of Christ. Pride and self have all of man, till man has his all from Christ. He, therefore, only fights the good fight that the selfish nature from Adam may be brought to death by the supernatural humility of Christ brought to life in him." – W. Law, Address to the Clergy, p. 52.

NOTE C

"To die to self, or come under its power, cannot be done by any active resistance we can make to it by the powers of nature. The one true way of dying to self is the way of patience, meekness, humility, and resignation to God. This is the truth and perfection of dying to self. For if I ask you what the Lamb of God means, you will tell me that it is the perfection of patience, meekness, humility, and resignation to God. Must you not, therefore, say that a desire and faith of these virtues is an application to Christ, is a giving up yourself to Him and the perfection of faith in Him?

And then, because this desire of your heart to sink down in patience, meekness, humility, and resignation to God, is truly giving up all that you are and have from Adam, it is leaving all you have to follow Christ; it is your highest act of faith in Him. Christ is nowhere but in these virtues; when they are there, He is in His own kingdom. Let this be the Christ you follow.

"The Spirit of divine love can have no place in any fallen creature, until it wants and chooses to be dead to all self, in a patient, humble resignation to the power and mercy of God.

"I seek for my salvation through the meek, humble, patient, suffering Lamb of God, who alone has the power to bring these heavenly virtues in my soul. There is no possibility of salvation except through the meek, humble, patient, resigned Lamb of God in our souls. When the Lamb of God has brought His own meekness, humility, and full resignation to God in our souls, then it is the birthday of the Spirit of love in our souls, which will feed our souls with such peace and joy in God that we will not remember anything that we called peace or joy before.

"This way to God is perfect. This perfection is grounded in the two-fold character of our Saviour: 1. He is the Lamb of God, a principle of all meekness and humility in the soul. 2. He is the Light of heaven, and blesses eternal nature, and turns it into a kingdom of heaven. When we are willing to find rest for our souls in meek and humble resignation to God, then as the Light of God and heaven, He joyfully breaks in, turns our darkness into light, and begins that kingdom of God and of love within us, which will never have an end." – See Wholly For God, pp 84-102.

NOTE D

"A Secret of Secrets: Humility the Soul of True Prayer.— Until the spirit of the heart is renewed, until it is emptied of all earthly desires, and stands in hunger and thirst after God —which is the true spirit of prayer—all our prayer will be too much like lessons given to scholars. We will mostly say them because we dare not neglect them. But do not be discouraged. Take the following advice, and then you may go to church without any danger of mere lip service or hypocrisy, even if there is a hymn or prayer whose language is higher than your heart.

Do this: go to the church as the tax collector went to the temple. Stand in the spirit of your mind as he outwardly expressed when he cast down his eyes and could only say, 'God be merciful to me, a sinner,' (Luke 18:13). Stand fixed in this state of heart. It will sanctify every prayer that comes out of your mouth.

When anything is read or sung or prayed that is more exalted than your heart is, make this an occasion of further sinking down in the spirit of the tax collector. You will then be helped, and highly blessed by those prayers and praises which seem only to belong to a heart better than yours.

This, my friend, is a secret of secrets. It will help you to reap where you have not sown, and be a continual source of grace in your soul. For everything that inwardly stirs in you, or outwardly happens to you, becomes a real good to you, if it excites this humble state of mind in you. For nothing is in vain, or without profit to the humble soul.

It stands always in a state of divine growth; everything that falls upon it is like a dew of heaven to it. Shut up yourself, therefore, in this form of Humility. All good is enclosed in it; it is a water of heaven, that turns the fire of the fallen soul into the meekness of the divine life, and creates that oil, out of which the love to God and man gets its flame.

Always be enclosed in it—let it be a garment that always covers you and a belt with which you are fastened. Only breathe in and from its spirit, only see with its eyes, only hear with its ears. And then, whether you are in or out of the church, hearing the praises of God or receiving wrongs from men and the world, all will be edification, and everything will help forward your growth in the life of God." – The Spirit of Prayer, Pt. II. p. 121.

www.ingramcontent.com/pod-product-compliance
Lightning Source LLC
LaVergne TN
LVHW020425070526
838199LV00003B/282